D1784875

# POLO

Copyright © Medibel S.A. 1997

All rights reserved under international copyright conventions. No part of this publication may be reproduced in any form or by any means without the prior permission in writing from the publisher.

ISBN 3-8238-1638-1

PHOTOGRAPHY CREDITS

Vicky Aguirre: Pages 4, 5, 28, 54 (bottom middle), 57 (left top and bottom), 62, 69, 73 (left top and bottom), 76, 77, 84, 85, 86, 88, 96, 97

Godfrey Argent: Page 112

Yann Arthus-Bertrand: Pages 2/3

Jonathan Becker: Page 12

Melito Cerezo: Pages 65, 73 (left), 80, 81, 83, 89, 90 (right)

Reto Guntli: Page 186

Paolo Koch: pages 6, 20, 21, 25, 27, 35, 53, 54 (top, and bottom left and right), 56, 58, 59, 66, 75 (right top and bottom), 78, 79, 82, 90 (left), 92/93, 94, 95, 98, 105, 109, 118 (right), 132, 133, 141, 146, 147, 153, 160, 163, 168, 169, 170, 171, 172, 173, 174, 176, 177, 178, 179, 180, 181, 182, 183, 184/185, 189, 190, 193, 194, 198/199, 202, 204, 205, 206, 208

David Lominska: Pages 1, 8, 14, 17, 22, 23, 24, 26, 29, 30, 31, 32, 33, 34, 36, 37, 38, 39, 40, 41, 42, 43, 44, 45, 46, 47, 48, 49, 50, 51, 52, 55, 57 (right), 87, 91, 106, 136, 137, 138, 144 (right top and bottom), 145 (bottom left), 151, 152, 154, 155, 156, 157, 158, 159, 161, 164, 165, 166, 167, 175

Mike Roberts: Pages 10, 18, 74 (top), 101, 102, 110/111, 115, 116, 118 (left), 120, 121, 122, 123, 124, 125, 126, 127, 128, 129, 130, 131, 134, 135, 142, 145 (top left), 148, 149, 150, 200, 201, 203

Dudu von Thielmann: Page 61

Ramon Tolosa: Pages 72 (right), 73 (right), 74 (bottom)

Courtesy Susan Barrantes: Pages 70, 113, 117, 119, 144 (left), 197

Courtesy Lord Patrick Beresford: Page 114

Courtesy Juan MacDonough: Page 60

Courtesy Negro Torres Zavaleta: Pages 72 (left), 145 (right)

Distribution in Germany and Austria by te Neues Verlag GmbH & Co. KG, 47906 Kempen (booktrade) and Grund Genug Verlag und Werbe GmbH, 20355 Hamburg (special sales).

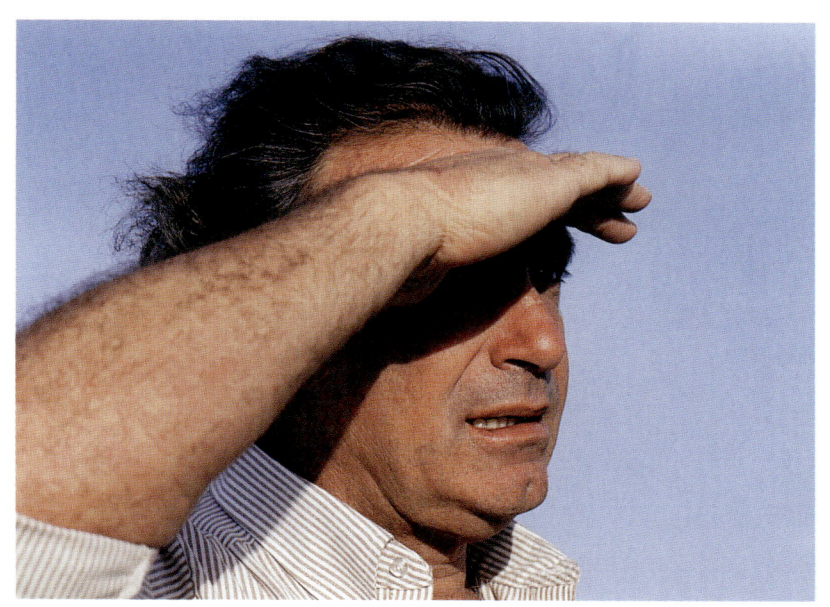

for Héctor

# POLO

### SUSAN BARRANTES

Foreword by H. R. H. The Prince of Wales

Introduction by Juan Carlos Harriot

# CONTENTS

When I first started playing polo over thirty years ago Susie Barrantes seemed to me to be a very important feature in the polo landscape. Apart from anything else, she displayed an incredible knowledge of all the details of the game and the breeding of the ponies. Her enthusiasm as a spectator in the stand was almost legendary, and she always seemed to know the rules of polo far better than any of the umpires... So this book will doubtless bring back many nostalgic memories for those who started playing polo in the 1950's or 1960's.

Her late husband, Hector Barrantes, was one of the great figures of the polo scene - in every sense of the word he was a big man. I remember him with immense affection and admiration as a true sportsman, a great team player and, above all, a wonderfully genial personality. The power of his hitting was remarkable and he frequently used to hit a ball from the centre of the ground so that it went over the back line, or straight through the goal. I count it a privilege to have played with him in the days when I could still take part in high goal polo and, like all his friends, I miss him enormously. The very least I can do, therefore, in his memory is to write this foreword to Susie's book as a personal tribute to Hector.

# INTRODUCTION

## by Juan Carlos Harriot

A S A SPORT, polo is hard, highly competitive, and full of risk. Beyond the game's obvious glamour and beauty is a hidden world of endless toil and effort. For these reasons, and for the tenacity, the character, and the cool mind it demands, I cannot conceive of polo as anything but a sport of gentlemen. The game, additionally, requires a noble sporting spirit, a sense of camaraderie, and—one need hardly say—a great love of horses.

Having read this book, I find it easy to understand the enthusiasm and affection with which Susan Barrantes has followed the sport of polo, the world of polo, and everything to do with horses. Her experience and knowledge, which can be found here on every page, have resulted in a volume that—like every great polo match—is both unique and unforgettable.

Juan Carlos Harriot in the library at Coronel Suárez, the estancia where he raises polo ponies. Photograph by Jonathan Becker.

# The Game of Polo

THE ORIGINS OF POLO go back to Persia, where there is evidence that an early form of the sport was played during the reign of Darius the Great, in the early sixth century B.C. The game spread to Constantinople and from there to Turkestan, Tibet, China, and Japan. It flourished in India during the Mogul empire, from the early sixteenth to the mid-eighteenth centuries. English officers in India took up the game, founded clubs, and formulated a set of rules. The Calcutta Polo Club, which has contributed so much to the development of the sport, was founded in the early 1860s, and from then on polo playing became an established part of the Anglo-Indian scene, passing to England at the end of the decade.

By the 1870s, polo in England was developing fast. The number of players per side was reduced from eight to four, and the duration of the game fixed at either six or eight seven-minute periods called chukkers. A clock times the period and a bell is rung to end each chukker. A warning bell is rung at seven minutes, after which the chukker continues—for up to an additional thirty seconds—until the ball goes out of play, or hits a board, or a foul is committed. A final bell is rung at seven and a half minutes, when play must stop immediately. In the

At Cowdray Park, polo ponies wait on the lines for their chance to join the game. Longtime professionals believe the animals watch the sport with as much interest as the human spectators. Each player needs several ponies for a game, which he changes between chukkers or, in an emergency, while play continues.

three-minute interval between chukkers, the players leave the ground and go to the lines to change their ponies.

Each player's performance is assessed and handicapped annually by a national commission composed of representatives from local clubs and members of national polo associations. A handicap can range from minus two to ten. Ten goals, the highest handicap, is awarded only to the best players. The figures refer not to the number of goals a player is expected to score but to his value to the team. The handicap of each team is the sum of the handicaps of its individual members. The handicap, then, becomes the scale by which tournaments are organized, so that matches are played only between teams with broadly similar ratings.

Most of polo's rules have developed to protect the players and ponies from accidents. The speed and contact of the game make it essential for a player to hold his stick in his right hand and control his pony with his left. The most important rules concern a player's "right of way." A player following directly in line behind the ball he has just hit has the right of way over other players; so does the player who is closest to the ball after it has been struck. Opponents are not allowed to cut in between players with the right of way and the ball. To prevent serious injury, the tactic of hooking sticks is governed by strict rules. Hooking is allowed only when a player is about to strike the ball. Reaching in front of an opponent's pony to hook sticks is considered a foul, as is hooking

The umpire holds the ball behind his back as the teams line up. To resume play, he will throw the ball down among the ponies' legs.

above shoulder level. Both are punished by granting a free hit to the opposing team from the thirty-, forty-, or sixty-yard line. There is no offside rule in polo.

The four-member team consists of a number one, the forward, who is responsible for scoring goals; a number two, who drives the ball into enemy territory; a number three, who works in the center of the ground and is the pivot of the team; and a back, number four, who takes charge of the defense. Players form rapid combinations, strike the ball with a mallet, and ride off their opponents by moving alongside an opposing player and forcing him off the line of the ball. Each game is subject to the rules and to the control of two mounted umpires and a referee sitting on the sideline.

Behind the excitement and glamour of the competitions, the big matches, and the international tournaments there is another world of polo. The daily chores and dedication of grooms, exercisers, schoolers, farm workers, horse breakers, truck drivers, and, nowadays, air carriers are essential to the game. Skilled craftsmen—the farriers, the makers of boots, saddles, and sticks—are irreplaceable characters, linked in their love for ponies and polo.

Players charging after the ball at full speed is always an exciting sight.

Polo has been played in India since the sixteenth century. Here, in Delhi, a bugle player announces the chukkers.

RIGHT: A Delhi linesman signals to the referee after a goal is scored.

An umpire carries extra balls on his saddle. Made of willow roots or compressed plastic, the ball has a diameter of 3¼ inches and weighs about 4½ ounces.

RIGHT: An old clock times each chukker. The timekeeper is protected by a screen from wild balls.

Andy Busch takes a wide swing at a ball at Palm Beach.

Gonzalito, Gonzalo Pieres's son, rises out of the saddle for a high forehand drive. At fourteen, Gonzalito is already a two-goaler. In Argentina, junior players are handicapped like adults.

Héctor Barrantes, at Palm Beach, playing for White Birch Farm, hits a near-side backhander, while Christian Laprida comes up on his right.

Umpire Julian Hipwood throws the ball down for a free shot. Penalty lines are thirty, forty, and sixty yards from each goalpost.

LEFT: The boards stop the ball, but Tommy Wayman's pony flies over them, as Carlos Gracida gets ready to strike. Players can cross the boards or ricochet the ball off them during play. On grounds where the sidelines are simply marked on the grass, a ball rolls out of play.

Players ride with a strap on their upper leg when they have pulled a riding muscle.

RIGHT: Near a corner of the ground, a player—his pony straddling the boards—takes a wide swing at the ball.

Gonzalo Pieres changing ponies in the Argentine Open at Palermo. His groom holds them side by side for a quick change off.

Not wanting to lose a moment of the game, Memo Gracida changes ponies as rapidly as possible. The clock does not stop during a chukker unless a player is lying motionless on the ground.

Juan José Boote makes a classic under-the-neck shot.

OPPOSITE: Paul Withers, playing for Cowdray Park, hooking sticks with Chuy Baez, for Ipanema.

Julian Hipwood and Paul Withers riding off at Cowdray. Polo ponies are trained to bump or push opponents away from the line of the ball. Players are not allowed to ride off at angles dangerous to other riders or their ponies.

OPPOSITE: Hooking sticks can stop an opponent from scoring a goal.

Martin Gruss, for Pegasus, and Joe Wayne Barry, for Ellerston White, riding off. Players wear knee pads and helmets for protection in high-speed and dangerous play.

OPPOSITE: Howard Hipwood, in green, being ridden off from his right side at Palm Beach Polo and Country Club.

BOTH PAGES: Sebastián Merlos,
in the red helmet, and Anthony
Embiricos have a rough encounter
at Midhurst, West Sussex.

Héctor Barrantes scores a goal with a difficult near-side backhand stroke. The goalposts, eight yards apart, must be flexible to withstand collisions with the players or ponies. This goalpost is covered by wooden slats.

OPPOSITE: A spectacular fall of players and ponies at Palm Beach. Héctor Barrantes, for White Birch Farm, hits the ground with his pony. Behind him, a player for Las Cachinas is also on the way down.

Eduardo Heguy hooks the stick of Max Gottschalk from below, thereby preventing him from striking the ball.

Stephan de Kwiatkowski and Jeff Hall riding off as they chase the ball.

A difficult under-the-belly shot executed by Andy Smith at Sun Valley, California.

Canes are flexible but do sometimes break, as in this under-the-neck shot by Bautista Heguy, playing for Ellerston White, in England. In Argentina, Bautista plays with his three brothers on the famous forty-goal Indios Chapaleufú I team.

ABOVE AND RIGHT: James Armstrong at Palm Beach, playing for Riverview, rises from his saddle to make an under-the-neck shot.

OPPOSITE: At sixteen, Gastón Moore, Eduardo Moore's nephew, is already a promising new player.

Jeff Blake and Owen Rinehart illustrate a perfect hooked-stick play at high speed. Hooking sticks is allowed only when an opponent is about to strike the ball.

OPPOSITE: Tim Fane on the ground, his boot and stick visible to the left, behind his fallen pony. His opponent, Adrian Wade, is also about to fall. Amazingly, nobody was hurt.

BOTH PAGES: Wicky el-Effendi, from Pakistan, collides with the goalpost at El Dorado Polo Club, Palm Springs, California. The pony turns left; el-Effendi, right.

The goalpost is uprooted. The short stick, which anchors the post, breaks in two behind the pony's rear hoof. The flag on top of the goalpost flies in the air, at right.

Billy Busch, at Palm Beach, playing for Ellerston White, illustrates a classic near-side backhander.

John Gobin, playing at Palm Beach for White Birch Farm, makes a difficult under-the-tail, backhand shot. Behind him, Billy Busch plays for Bud Light.

BOTH PAGES: Billy Busch, playing for White Birch Farm, in a slow-motion fall.

An umpire at Palm Beach communicates by signal with another umpire.

LEFT: An umpire watches, at right, as a high ball flies over the players' heads.

TOP ROW: Plaited tails: (left) an American knot; (middle) a braid at Cowdray Park. If ponies' tails are not tied up, a player might catch his stick in the tail and break his wrist. A fringed headband (right) keeps flies away from a pony's eyes; a muzzle prevents the pony from eating its bed.

BOTTOM ROW: Legs: (left) a traditional Argentine *potro*, or pony-skin boot; (middle) colorful bandages protect the pony's legs during play; (right) a Nigerian umpire wears traditional clogs.

OPPOSITE: Grooms wash off ponies after a game.

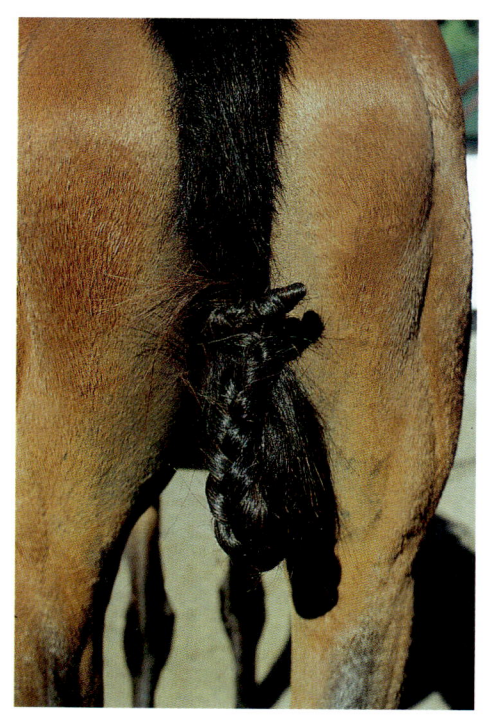

Ian Compton cuts leather for polo saddles at Calcutt's, in Sutton Scotney, England.

OPPOSITE: Champions' saddles— buckskin saddles with overgirths belonging to ten-goalers Gonzalo Pieres and Horacio Santiago Heguy.

OPPOSITE, FAR RIGHT: A tackman carries four saddles to the pony lines.

Fagliano's, the most famous boot maker in Argentina, makes polo players' boots at Hurlingham, Buenos Aires.

OPPOSITE:
Villamil, at Hurlingham, Buenos Aires, makes world-famous polo mallets. The measuring stick leaning against the bench determines the length of each mallet, usually from forty-nine to fifty-four inches, depending on the height of the pony. Players take a collection of favorite mallets of varying weights and lengths to each game.

Juan Mac Donough and his company, Unicorn, transport polo ponies worldwide. Here, four ponies wait to be hoisted into a plane.

Starting in the early eighties, several major airlines began to transport polo ponies. Loaded on their pallets inside the plane, the ponies enjoy an air-conditioned trip.

OPPOSITE: In a cloud of dust, a truck transports Ellerstina's ponies back home to Pilar Chico, Argentina, after a game.

# Polo in Argentina

As a young girl who grew up in a world of horses, I saw the rebirth of the game of polo in England after the Second World War but not until I first came to Argentina with an English team, in 1966, did I begin to understand the sport's true nature. In Argentina at that time, the top teams were legendary. The ponies, which could stop, spin on a coin, and then shoot off at full speed, demonstrated in every game why Argentine polo ponies were considered the best in the world.

There is something very special about the number one ground in the district of Palermo, Buenos Aires, known to everyone simply as Palermo. The setting, with its great green rectangle surrounded by skyscrapers and stands, is a perfect frame for the magnificent spectacle. Every polo player's greatest ambition is to play here, in the heart of the city, opposite the Argentine Hippodrome, on Avenue Libertador, one of the city's main thoroughfares. Ground number one has been the scene of some of the world's greatest polo games. It was at Palermo, in the classic finals between the Coronel Suárez and Santa Ana teams, that I first saw Argentine polo played brilliantly. Here, in the midst of players avidly discussing the game with polo heroes of earlier decades, and surrounded by

The most famous polo ground in the world, the number one ground at Palermo, Buenos Aires, where the Argentine Open Championship is held every November, holds 15,000 spectators and is 300 yards long by 200 yards wide. This aerial view includes the Hippodrome racetrack (top left), the center of Buenos Aires (top right), the River Plate, and, in the distance, the coast of Uruguay.

the less critical admiration of the general public out to enjoy a day in the sun, I felt part of a ritual, an act that was a way of life in Argentina.

A decade later, in the seventies, I was often at Palermo as a fervent supporter of my husband's team, Nueva Escocia, and I watched magnificent strokes, breathtaking falls, and memorable games. To see this remarkable sport, this strong, swift game, in these surroundings is a unique experience. Nor does it end there, for, after the game, it is wonderful to go to the bar under the central stand and take part in the cross fire of praise and criticism of the players and the ponies. Here, in the atmosphere of a first night at the theater, old friends get together and comment on the game or meet people who live in the country and only come to Palermo once a year for this occasion.

Although the English had a lot to do with bringing polo to Argentina at the end of the nineteenth century, local players soon became very skilled. The Argentine Polo Association was founded in 1922, and Argentina rose rapidly to international status, winning the Olympic Gold Medal at the Paris games, in 1924, and again in Berlin, in 1936. During the forties and fifties, two teams were in constant battle for pride of place. El Trébol won the Argentine Open Championship for four consecutive years, when the team was made up of two famous pairs of

The two Heguy teams, Indios Chapaleufú I and II, line up with two umpires before the finals of the Argentine Open, in 1996, with the tall buildings of Buenos Aires in the background. Chapaleufú II, in the dark red shirts on the right, became the new champions.

brothers, Luis and Heriberto Duggan and Carlos and Julio Menditeguy. At first their handicaps ranged from four to six, but they soon realized that the caliber of their ponies would prove to be the key factor in improving their game. Shortly after the Menditeguys trained new ponies, the team was playing off a handicap of thirty-nine goals. Their game was neater and their passing more exact than that of any other team. They were invincible.

The brothers Enrique and Juan Carlos Alberdi and cousins Juan and Roberto Cavanagh formed the Venado Tuerto team, which played against El Trébol four times in the Open and finally, in 1944, succeeded in defeating them. The same team of Alberdis and Cavanaghs went on to win the Open for three consecutive years between 1946 and 1948, and again in 1955. Their powerful playing style—dominating and physical—was very different from the style of their opponents and it resulted in memorable and historic encounters.

The Coronel Suárez team, which became the unbeatable champions at Palermo in the sixties and seventies, blended the strengths of El Trébol and Venado Tuerto and also injected tremendous speed into the game. Coronel Suárez, made up of the Heguy brothers, Horacio and Alberto Pedro, and the Harriot brothers, Juan Carlos, Jr., and Alfredo, won the Open six times in succession and twelve times in all. Between 1957 and 1964, Juan Carlos Harriot, Jr., played seven times on the winning Coronel Suárez team with his father, Juan Carlos Harriot, Sr., and

The Coronel Suárez team dominated polo in Argentina in the sixties and seventies. Here, in the dark red-and-blue shirts they ride to the ground in Buenos Aires with their opponents, Mar del Plata, in light blue. To avoid injury, players must always hold their sticks in their right hands.

went on to win the Open twenty times in all. In these years, the Santa Ana team, with the Dorignac brothers, Gastón and Francisco, Daniel González, and Héctor Merlos, was Coronel Suárez's classic rival. Santa Ana played strong, aggressive polo, winning the Open in 1971, with Téofilo (Totti) Bordeu in place of Merlos, in 1973, and again, in 1982, with Guillermo Gracida, Jr., in place of González. Between them, these two teams modernized Argentina's traditional style of playing the game.

After the legendary era of Corónel Suarez, the eighties at Palermo were dominated by La Espadaña, which benefited from a new generation of superb players, such as the brothers Alfonso and Gonzalo Pieres, Ernesto Trotz, Jr., and Carlos Gracida. From 1984 to 1990, with the exception of 1986, La Espadaña won every Open and became the classic champions of the decade.

From 1986 and into the nineties, the Indios Chapaleufú team, made up of three and then four Heguy brothers—Marcos, Gonzalo, his twin, Horacio, Jr., and Bautista—brought new dynamism and dash to the game. They won the Open in 1986, 1991, 1992, 1993, and 1995. In 1994, Gonzalo Pieres and his teammate Carlos Gracida won the Open playing for Ellerstina, with two new young players, Adolfo Cambiaso, Jr., and Mariano Aguerre. In 1996, a second Heguy team, Indios Chapaleufú II, won the Open. This team consisted of Alejandro Díaz

The board at Hurlingham lists these high-goal players in the order of their positions on the team. Each name is followed by the player's handicap.

Alberdi and three brothers, Alberto (Pepe), Ignacio (Nachi), and Eduardo Heguy—first cousins of the Indios Chapaleufú I players.

There is no doubt that Argentina's international success in polo derives from the naturalness with which Argentines practice the sport and from their handing down of the game's secrets. On *estancias*, Argentina's huge country estates, children learn to understand and handle ponies at an early age. Riding and schooling ponies, stick and balling, and practice games in the summer are part of daily life.

At the hundredth anniversary of the Hurlingham Polo Club, founded in 1888 by the British in Argentina, four old opponents line up with Susan Barrantes. These veteran polo champions are (left to right) Julio Menditeguy, who played for El Trébol; Juan Cavanagh and his cousin Roberto Cavanagh, who played for Venado Tuerto; and Heriberto (Pepe) Duggan, of El Trébol.

H. R. H. The Duke of Edinburgh, a five-goaler, came to Argentina with the Commonwealth team in 1966. Here he prepares for a game of country polo with the leading Argentine players of the sixties, Juan Carlos Harriot, José María (Negro) Torres Zavaleta, and his twin, Jorge.

Members of the famous Coronel Suárez team show off their cup after winning the Open at Palermo. The classic team was made up of two pairs of brothers, from left to right, Alberto Pedro Heguy, Juan Carlos and Alfredo Harriot, and Horacio Heguy.

La Espadaña team in 1984 consisted of Ernesto Trotz, Gonzalo Pieres, Alfonso Pieres, and Juan Martín Zavaleta.

Winners of the Belgrano Cup in 1978 at Coronel Suárez, José María Azumendi, Roberto James, Gonzalo Tanoira, and Héctor Barrantes, playing for the Trenque Lauquen team.

Eduardo Moore in 1978 with two famous ponies, Fabiola and Lass.

BELOW: The champion Santa Ana team in 1973 after winning the Open. Team members (left to right) are Francisco Dorignac, Daniel González, Héctor Merlos, and Gastón Dorignac.

CLOCKWISE FROM TOP LEFT:
Alberto Pedro Heguy, Horacio's brother, a veteran of a great polo-playing dynasty in Argentina.

Ten-goaler Gonzalo Tanoira cooling off between chukkers. His team, Mar del Plata, was a strong competitor at Palermo in the seventies. Members included his brother Jorge Tanoira, Alfredo (Negro) Goti, and Alec Mihanovich.

In the seventies, Juan Carlos Harriot (left) and Horacio Heguy (right) played for the unbeatable Coronel Suárez team along with brothers Alfredo Harriot and Alberto Heguy.

Alfonso Pieres, a ten-goaler, carries his sticks to the ground.

CLOCKWISE FROM TOP LEFT:
Teammates on Kerry Packer's
team Ellerstina—Carlos Gracida
(a ten-goaler), Adolfo Cambiaso,
Jr., (a ten-goaler), Gonzalo Pieres
(a ten-goaler), and Mariano Aguerre
(a nine-goaler). The team won
the Argentine Open in 1994.

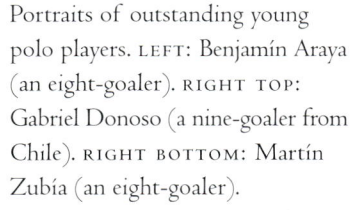

Portraits of outstanding young polo players. LEFT: Benjamín Araya (an eight-goaler). RIGHT TOP: Gabriel Donoso (a nine-goaler from Chile). RIGHT BOTTOM: Martín Zubía (an eight-goaler).

Before the Argentine Open at Palermo in 1980, the Coronel Suárez team sits on the sidelines. From left to right—Benjamín Araya, Alberto Pedro Heguy, Alfredo Harriot, and Celestino Garrós. The renowned Coronel Suárez team, consisting of two Heguys and two Harriots, broke up that year, but with two new players, Araya and Garrós, the team still won the Open.

After winning the game, the re-formed Coronel Suárez team of Araya, Heguy, Harriot, and Garrós, surrounded by young admirers, holds the silver Open Championship Cup.

The Indios Chapaleufú I team, a maximum-handicap, forty-goal team, consists of four Heguy brothers—Bautista, Gonzalo, Horacio, Jr., and Marcos.

The Indios Chapaleufú II team, sponsored by Asprey, won the Argentine Open in 1996. The team members are Eduardo Heguy, Alejandro Díaz Alberdi, Ignacio Heguy, and Alberto Heguy, Jr.

Traditional Argentine riding clothes include *bombachas* (the pleated britches), a wide leather belt studded with silver coins, worn low on the hips, often with a sheathed knife tucked in at the back, and a broad-brimmed hat. Here, elegant in his best riding gear, a groom waits with a pony.

OPPOSITE: At the 1996 semi-finals at Palermo, the Ellerstina team is listed with its very high handicap of thirty-nine. The letter H after Adolfo Cambiaso's name stands for *hijo* (son or Jr.).

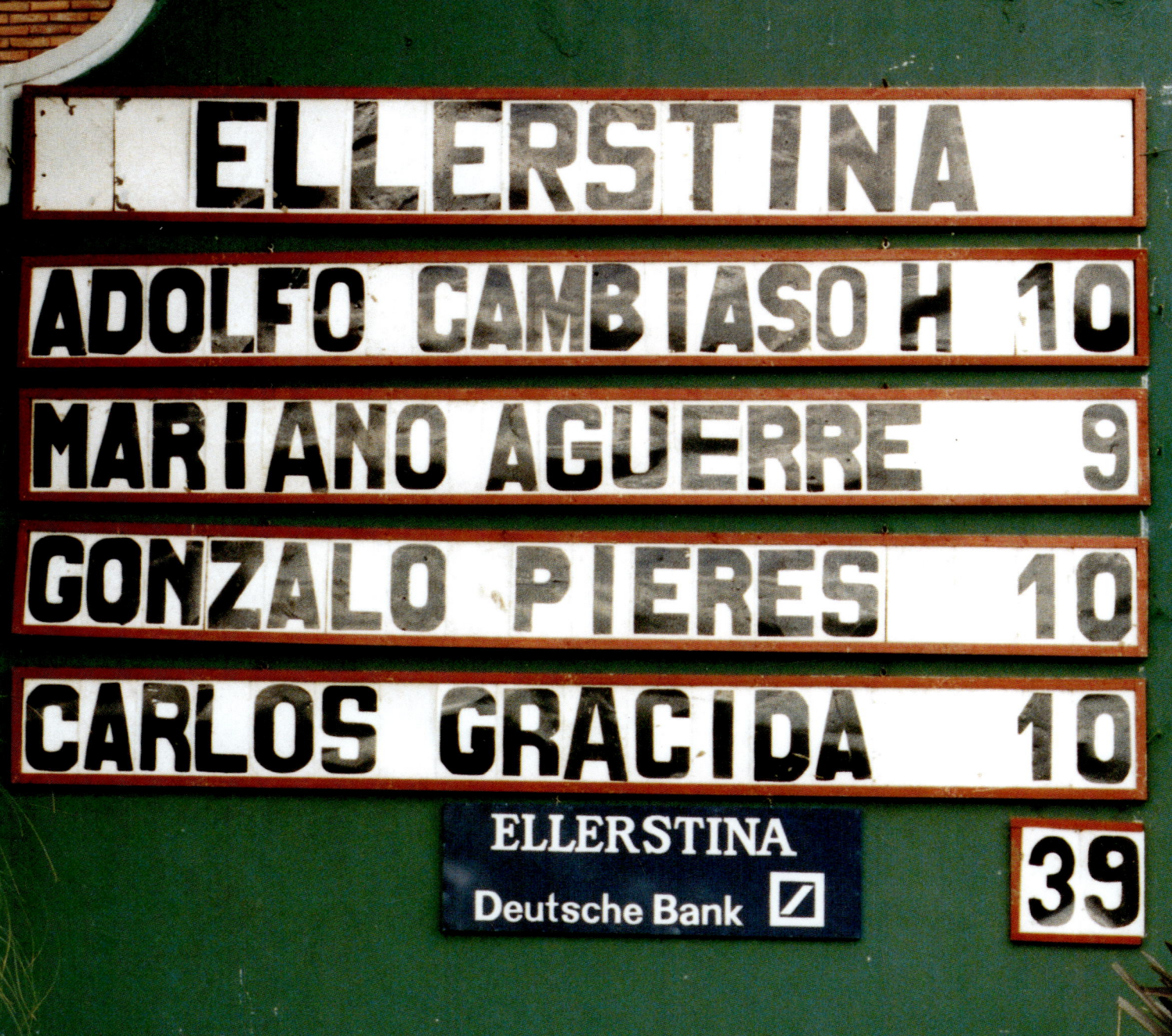

Gonzalo Pieres (right), playing
for La Espadaña, rides off Horacio
Heguy, Jr., (left), playing for
the original Indios Chapaleufú,
in Tortugas, Argentina.

Eduardo Heguy and Adolfo Cambiaso race for the ball at Palermo. Moving at thirty-five miles an hour, a polo player must aim for a ball that measures three and a quarter inches in diameter.

Marcos Heguy hooks sticks at the gallop.

OPPOSITE: Benjamín Araya, playing number three, leans out and hooks sticks with Mariano Aguerre.

Alberto (Pepe) Heguy playing for Indios Chapaleufú II.

Hubert Perrodo, a French player and patron of the team Château Labégorce, also the name of his Bordeaux vineyard, plays at Pilar Chico. His team is usually based either at Windsor or Deauville.

The sons of players in the Argentine Open at Palermo practice polo on foot behind the stands.

Gonzalito Pieres, now a two-goaler, stick and balling on his motorbike.

OPPOSITE: Young players ride adult-sized ponies and use adult-sized sticks.
Facundo Pieres, the younger brother of Gonzalito, is ten years old.

In front of Los Indios clubhouse, near Buenos Aires, two young teams prepare to play for the Potrillos Cup in 1980. *Potrillos*, meaning young foals, is the name affectionately given to this junior trophy.

Inside the stables at the Hurlingham Club. The first polo club in Argentina, Hurlingham was founded by British players. Soon after, the game was adopted enthusiastically and skillfully by Argentines.

RIGHT: Behind the scenes at Hurlingham, polo ponies wait for the day's schooling.

At La Lechuza, Gonzalo Pieres's stables in Pilar Chico, Pieres (right) and his friend Open champion veteran Teófilo (Totti) Bordeu discuss the condition of ponies preparing for the tournaments. In Argentina such discussions are usually accompanied by the drinking of maté, a traditional Argentine herbal tea.

LEFT: The Ellerstina stables at Pilar Chico, near Buenos Aires, were built by Peter Brant and are now owned by Kerry Packer. Preparing for the Open, Juan José Boote schools his faithful friend, the prize-winning pony Luna, for her player Gonzalo Pieres.

# Polo in England

IN THE FIFTIES, English polo was a weekend game played on large country estates by people who did not make great demands on themselves and were mainly interested in amusement. Prewar English polo had been of a considerable standard, but now only a few of its leading figures remained. Among these were Humphrey Guinness, Gerald Balding, and David Dawnay. After the war, polo consisted simply of groups of friends getting together with just two or four ponies—animals they had had since 1939. Games lasted for a few chukkers only, and playing mattered more than the results. Since those days, I have witnessed this homegrown polo gradually evolve. By attracting players from other countries and by changing some of the rules, English polo has become a fully professional sport.

During the sixties and seventies, as more and more Argentine players and grooms went to England, the game there gained new strength. The English changed their training methods. The ponies lost their stocky build and were schooled in a different way. Gradually Argentine influences improved both play and ponies, so that the seventies saw the emergence of such fine players as Paul Withers; the Beresford brothers, the Marquess of Waterford and

On the Long Walk at Windsor Castle, two young grooms take polo ponies to the Smith's Lawn polo ground. In the fifties and sixties, the Windsor Park team played an important part in encouraging the revival of polo in England.

Lord Patrick Beresford; and Ronald Ferguson; and later, the Hipwood brothers, Julian and Howard, and Alan Kent. Soon teams from Italy, Spain and, towards the end of the seventies, North America began to appear on the scene.

While Argentine polo players were having a crucial influence on the development of English polo, they were not professionals. Many sold ponies to pay for the journey to Europe and their upkeep in England. Little by little, the reputation of their ponies and their schooling methods inspired such interest that Argentines began to concentrate on selling their ponies to the English. The first Argentine player to go to England at this time was Tito Lalor. I vividly remember seeing him play at Friar Park, near Henley-on-Thames, in 1957, as it was the first game of polo I had ever watched. Lalor was playing with Archie David, who was then the strength of the Windsor Park team, mounting the team with his excellent ponies. Tito went on to play in England for many years. After him came Wyndham Lacey, Rojas Lanusse, and Eduardo Moore, who sold more ponies than any one else at the time. Lacey and Lanusse played in Boyd-Gibbins' team at Silverleys, in Bishops Stortford, Hertfordshire. Arthur Lucas, who founded the club and polo team at Woolmers Park, in Hertfordshire, brought over many Argentine players. All these men were pioneers.

There were a number of excellent English teams in the seventies. One of the best was Claire and Simon

Drum horse and trumpeters of the Household Cavalry before the Coronation Cup at Smith's Lawn, Windsor.

Tomlinson's Los Locos. Claire, the daughter of Arthur Lucas, was the only woman to attain a five-goal handicap and to play high-level polo. She always had Argentine grooms and is one of the few people in England to breed and train her own polo ponies. Today she has a club near Cirencester.

The seventies saw the advent of the famous Stowell Park team. Its members were the two Vestey brothers, Sam and Mark, Eduardo Moore, and Héctor Barrantes, who led and trained the team. Throughout the decade, they won a series of victories that made them the most successful team in England. In 1973 and 1975 they won every match in the high- and medium-handicap tournaments, and their record remains unbeaten. As a result, the Hurlingham Polo Association raised their handicaps, until Moore was rated at ten, Barrantes at nine, and Sam and Mark Vestey at four each. As the maximum allowable handicap for a team in England was twenty-two goals, they had to split up. Eduardo Moore and Mark Vestey formed the Foxcote team, while Sam Vestey and Héctor Barrantes continued with Stowell Park. Both teams were very successful until the outbreak of the South Atlantic War, in 1982, an event that prevented the Argentines from returning to England.

I would say that Stowell Park rose to the top because year after year it was able to keep the same players, grooms, ponies, and veterinary surgeons. The systematic way the team was run was an essential factor in

Between two glowing fields of rape, polo ponies are led from their farm to the Guards' Polo Club at Windsor Park.

maintaining its high-quality performance. When players work steadily together with the same people, over time they learn each pony's habits and preferences, even such small details as where a pony likes to stand in the stable. All this accumulated knowledge and the continuity of routine are important to the smooth running of a team.

I make no claim to mention all those who played a part in raising postwar English polo to an international level but wish only to describe some of the steps in this evolution. The sport was in a critical state when Lord Cowdray came on the scene after the war and, with tireless energy, began to promote the game. With three of his five sisters and his brother-in-law, John Lakin, Lord Cowdray launched the first tournament to be held at Cowdray Park. Instituted in 1949 as the Challenge Cup, the competition provided the springboard for an English team to go to Buenos Aires. The team consisted of Bob Skene, John Traill, Peter Dollar, and Humphrey Guinness. Though defeated by Argentina, they re-established England's place in international competition. Another important consequence of the trip was Lord Cowdray's purchase of more than fifty Argentine ponies, which for many years formed the nucleus of animals in his club. Not only did Lord Cowdray revive English polo by his generosity but he also managed to make Cowdray Park the center of European polo. After 1956, when he founded the Gold Cup, to win at Cowdray Park became a major achievement and attracted internationally famous players, thereby

Lord Cowdray, an enthusiastic polo player and promoter, made Cowdray Park the home of renewed interest in polo in the fifties. In this aerial photograph, the ruins of the old castle are visible on the right, and the number one ground, the Lawns, lined with spectators' cars before a game, stretches from the far left to the center.

adding to the reputation of the English game. From Argentina came Juan Carlos Harriot, Carlos Menditeguy, Daniel González, Horacio Heguy, José María Torres Zavaleta, Horacio Baibiene, Alec Mihanovich, Juan José Díaz Alberdi, Héctor Merlos, and Horacio and Benjamín Araya. From the United States came John Oxley, Hap Sharp, Chico and Roy Barry, Peter Perkins, Red Armour, Tommy Wayman, and Billy Linfoot. India was represented by Rao Rajah Hanut Singh and Prem Singh. Sinclair Hill came from Australia, and Pablo Rincón Gallardo, Antonio Herrera, and two generations of the Gracida family from Mexico.

In 1966, Lord Cowdray took the British Commonwealth Team to Buenos Aires, where they met the Argentine national team and the United States team. The Commonwealth team consisted of the Duke of Edinburgh, the Marquess of Waterford, his brother Lord Patrick Beresford, Ronald Ferguson, Paul Withers, Patrick Kemple, from Rhodesia, and Sinclair Hill, from Australia. Rao Rajah Hanut Singh was in charge of the ponies. The team had considerable success against the United States, but the Argentines were the undisputed victors. Although the Duke of Edinburgh was only in Argentina for a short time, his presence gave the championship great distinction. I also remember watching him play a very good game at the Hurlingham Club, near Buenos Aires, as a member of Daniel González's team.

Polo ponies wait their turn on the lines at Windsor.

The Duke of Edinburgh has played a very important role in English polo. A five-goal player, he was tough, enthusiastic, and competitive. His participation gave the game tremendous prestige, and large numbers of people flocked to see the matches in which he played. In the sixties he led a successful team, called Windsor Park, the only English side ever to win the Gold Cup. Besides the prince, other members of Windsor Park were Lord Patrick Beresford, his brother, the Marquess of Waterford, and Paul Withers, who played back.

The Prince of Wales also increased the popularity of polo. For many years he successfully took part in medium- and high-goal games. Together with Julian Hipwood, the best English player, the prince played for Guy Wildenstein's team, Diables Bleus. Thereafter he played for Galen Weston's Maple Leafs and later for Geoffrey Kent's Windsor Park.

An excited crowd of spectators runs to see the trophy presented after the Coronation Cup finals at Windsor.

H. R. H. The Prince of Wales (left) and the Duke of Edinburgh, playing for Windsor Park, prepare to strike the ball at Windsor in the sixties.

Polo players from four continents on the famous Eric Moller team after winning the medium-goal Harrison Cup at Cowdray in 1964. From left to right, Patrick Kemple, from Rhodesia; Eric Moller, from England; Rao Rajah Hanut Singh, from India; and Ricardo Díaz, from Argentina.

OPPOSITE: Prince Charles at Windsor in 1980 prepares to play for Diables Bleus with the help of his groom, Osvaldo Pineda.

In 1969 the Gold Cup was again won by Windsor Park, in a close 7-6 game—the only time the cup was won by an entirely English team. From left to right—their opponents, playing for Pimm's, are Brian Bethel, Daniel González, the Earl of Brecknock, and Héctor (Cacho) Merlos; Windsor Park was represented by Paul Withers, the Duke of Edinburgh, the Marquess of Waterford, and Lord Patrick Beresford.

The Cowdray Park Gold Cup was won in 1966 by the Windsor Park team. Archie David (center front) an ex-Windsor Park player and benefactor, presents the cup. From left to right— the Cowdray Park team of Sinclair Hill, Robert Cudmore, Alec Harper, and Michael Hare (now Lord Blakenham); and the winning Windsor Park team of Gonzalo Tanoira, the Duke of Edinburgh, the Marquess of Waterford, and his brother, Lord Patrick Beresford.

OPPOSITE: Lord Charles Beresford demonstrates a classic under-the-neck near-side backhander.

The powerful Stowell Park team dominated English polo in the seventies. Here, in 1975, they admire the Gold Cup they have just won. From left to right— Mark Vestey, Eduardo Moore, Kate Vestey, Héctor Barrantes, and Lord Vestey.

OPPOSITE: Lord Vestey (far left) and Eduardo Moore (far right) play for Stowell Park against Patrick Churchward and Paul Withers (center) for Cowdray Park.

Ronnie Driver, captain of the Flamingos, receives a cup from Queen Elizabeth, The Queen Mother.

Lord Vestey enjoying his victory.

After the unbeatable Stowell Park team broke up in 1975, its old team members assembled outside Stowell Park House to display the hoard of cups they won in their last season together. From left to right—Lord Vestey (Stowell Park), Eduardo Moore and Mark Vestey (Foxcote), and Héctor Barrantes (Stowell Park). Their winnings are, again left to right, the high-goal Queen's Cup, the medium-goal County Cup, the high-goal Warwickshire Cup, the medium-goal Harrison Cup, and the high-goal Gold Cup.

120

John Horswell makes an acrobatic under-the-tail shot.

OPPOSITE: Her Majesty The Queen presents the Coronation Cup at Smith's Lawn, Windsor, in 1975, to the winners of the England vs. Argentina game. It was the first time England had played for the cup in many years. The Argentine team members were, from left to right, Héctor Barrantes, J. J. Díaz Alberdi, Eduardo Moore, and Gonzalo Pieres. Next to the Queen is John Wilson, chairman of W. D. and H. O. Wills, sponsor of the cup, and in the background are the Prince of Wales (center) and Lord Mountbatten (right).

Gonzalo Pieres is congratulated
by the Duke of Edinburgh
after winning the Coronation
Polo Cup in 1975.

RIGHT: Chris Bethel and
Mike Azzaro.

Contenders for the Pimm's Cup at Windsor, the Prince of Wales played for Maple Leafs, Henryk de Kwiatkowski and Robert Hyssam for Kwiatkowski's winning Kennelot team.

Her Majesty The Queen congratulates Kerry Packer and his team, Ellerston White, winners of the Queen's Cup in 1994 at the Guards' Polo Club, Windsor.

H. R. H. The Duchess of York, accompanied by H. R. H. The Duke of York, presents the Queen's Cup to Guy Wildenstein and his team, Diables Bleus, in 1986, at Smith's Lawn, Windsor.

Guy Wildenstein's team, Diables Bleus, won the Queen's Cup in 1986. From left to right—the Prince of Wales, Robert Graham, Julian Hipwood, and Guy Wildenstein.

Carlos Gracida competes against Alejandro Díaz Alberdi in the Gold Cup at Cowdray. With a good swing, a player can drive the ball up to 160 yards.

In the Autumn Tournament of the Guards' Polo Club, Charles Beresford plays for Santa Fe at Smith's Lawn, Windsor.

OPPOSITE: Antonio Herrera, playing for Flamingos, pursuing the ball at top speed.

Mike Rutherford of the rock group Mike and the Mechanics is also a keen polo player.

RIGHT: Claire Tomlinson, the world's leading woman polo player, and her husband, Simon, in the colors of their team, Los Locos, compete at the Guards' Club.

OPPOSITE: Emma Tomlinson, in the green helmet, daughter of Claire and Simon Tomlinson, is already a promising young player at fifteen. Howard Smith, eighteen, rides up behind her.

Polo is also a spectator sport enjoyed on a summer's afternoon by the whole family.

H. R. H. The Princess of Wales
presents Galen Weston with the
Warwickshire Cup for his team,
Maple Leafs, at Cirencester, in 1985.

The Coronation Cup is presented to the winning English team by the Princess of Wales, in 1988. From left to right—Peter Thwaites, president of the English Polo Association, Andrew Seavill, Julian Hipwood, the Princess, the team's sponsor Alain Dominique Perrin, president of Cartier, John Horswell, and Lord Charles Beresford.

Lord Cowdray replaces divots on the Lawns at Cowdray Park between chukkers.

RIGHT: Steaming ponies cool off after an energetic chukker at Cowdray Park.

# Polo in the USA and Elsewhere

IN THE UNITED STATES between 1960 and 1970, the appearance of a new generation of great players gave American polo a boost. Among the large number of talented North American professional players I have come to know are Red Armour, Tommy Wayman, Dale Smicklas, Walter Ray Harrington, Norty Knox, Peter Perkins, Mike Azzaro, and the entire Barry family. Before them came such legendary players as Stewart B. Iglehart, Robert Skene, Winston Guest, Thomas Hitchcock, Cecil Smith, and Michael Phipps.

At the outbreak of the South Atlantic War in 1982, when Argentine players had to leave England, polo in the United States was strengthened by the influx of top players—among them Alfonso Pieres, Eduardo Moore, and Héctor Barrantes—who went there to play and in turn attracted other international players. There was great activity in Palm Beach, Florida, and in Greenwich, Connecticut, where the main inspiration came from Peter Brant, who plays off a handicap of seven goals and has done much for American polo. His team, White Birch Farm, led by Gonzalo Pieres and Héctor Barrantes, became unbeatable. In the eighties, they won the East Coast Open in Boston, and every tournament in Palm Beach, Greenwich, and Saratoga. New polo centres appeared in

A view of the ground from the stands at the Eldorado Polo Club in Indio, California, with the San Jacinto mountains in the background. The Governor's Cup, held here every March, attracts the largest number of competing polo teams in the world.

States, among them the Palm Beach Polo and Country Club, in Wellington, Florida; the Retama Club, in San Antonio, Texas; and Boca Raton, in Florida, founded by John Oxley.

As polo became increasingly professional, beginning in the seventies, a new figure emerged—the polo patron. Rising costs and a new generation of young players with a different and very international approach to the sport began to make their influence felt. In America, in addition to Peter Brant, a leading new patron is Mrs. Helen Boehm, who never played polo but who financed the Boehm team in Palm Beach. Mickey Tarnopol has had a considerable impact with his team, Revlon, in Greenwich, Connecticut, and in Florida, as has Henryk de Kwiatkowski, with his team, Kennelot, also of Greenwich, Connecticut.

Among English polo patrons are Lord Vestey, his brother, Mark Vestey, and Galen Weston. One of the new mainstays of polo in England is Urs Schwarzenbach, with his team, Black Bears, which includes the brothers Sebastián and Juan Ignacio Merlos. The Australian Kerry Packer is another prominent patron and enthusiastic player. In spite of a multiple by-pass operation, Packer went on, with Gonzalo Pieres, to win the Gold Cup in 1995. Packer has built a fine club in England on the outskirts of Midhurst, West Sussex, and he owns well-appointed stables in Pilar Chico, near Buenos Aires, for his Argentine team, Ellerstina, as well as the famous team at his

In New Delhi, teams compete for the President's Cup. In the background is the Mogul tomb of Safdar Jung.

Ellerston club, in New South Wales, Australia. Germany, with main polo centers in Düsseldorf, Hamburg, and Munich, has a number of active clubs. The Hamburg club, founded in 1895, is the oldest in the country. Its most prominent player is Adi Darboven. The club in Munich, founded in 1985, boasts a spectacular alpine setting.

A leading patron in Asia is the Sultan of Brunei. At the end of the seventies, he founded his own club, with the help of Jack Williams, Eduardo Moore, and Héctor Barrantes, who supplied the first hundred ponies. Moore formed a team with the sultan and one of his brothers, Prince Jeffrey, while another brother, Prince Mohammed, and Barrantes made up a second team. Since then the club has become one of the foremost polo centers in the world. Brunei also sponsors the Argentine teams of Indios Chapaleufú I and II. The Crown Prince of Pahang, in Malaysia, is another prominent figure in present-day polo. His father, the Sultan of Pahang, is also a great enthusiast.

Corporate firms play an ever larger role in the sport. Some of those that support polo are Asprey, Cartier, Coca-Cola, Diners Club, Marlboro, MasterCard, Möet & Chandon, Revlon, and Rolex. Nowadays these names are always in evidence at international polo competitions.

A polo club was founded in St. Moritz, in Switzerland, in 1906 by some British cavalry officers. A polo tournament, organized by Reto Gaudenzi, a top Swiss player, has been held annually since 1985 on the frozen lake using a larger-than-usual yellow or orange ball, which is highly visible against the snow. There is also a summer polo tournament in Gstaad.

Baron Elie de Rothschild, a polo patron and generous host, with Héctor Barrantes and his pony after a game at Deauville in 1970.

RIGHT TOP: Tommy Wayman, a U.S. ten-goaler, gives last instructions to his son, Toby, before a game at Palm Beach.

RIGHT BOTTOM: Robert Skene, from Australia, a ten-goaler who played for U.S. teams.

After winning the Silver Cup at Deauville in the early seventies, Francisco Soldati, Daniel González, José María (Negro) Torres Zavaleta, and Michael Cárcano line up with their trophies and their enthusiastic supporter, the Maharanee of Jaipur, now the Rajmata.

LEFT TOP: The Crown Prince of Pahang, Tengku Mahkote, is, like his father, a high-level international polo player and promoter.

LEFT BOTTOM: Kerry Packer, an international backer of many different sports, plays for his team, Ellerston White, in Palm Beach.

In the sixties and seventies, at the end of the polo season in England, many English and international players continued to play across the Channel in a relaxed and social three-week polo season at Deauville, France. Here, Alex Ebeid, in the red helmet, patron of the Falcons, and his teammate Bautista Castilla (foreground) race their opponent, David Yeoman, for the ball.

OPPOSITE: One of the hazards of games at Deauville is the gulls that invade the ground during play.

Urs Schwarzenbach (left), a leading patron in England, with his team, Black Bears, sitting at halftime with their collection of mallets.

In 1968, the winning Boehm team at the Royal Berkshire Polo Club was made up of two sets of brothers. From left to right—Julian Hipwood, Carlos Gracida, Memo Gracida, the team patron Mrs. Helen Boehm, and Howard Hipwood.

Peter Brant, a leading American polo player and team sponsor, rides for his team, White Birch Farm, at Palm Beach Polo and Country Club, Florida.

OPPOSITE: The Meadowbrook Polo Club, in Bethpage, Long Island, was established in 1890 and is the oldest polo club in the United States. The U.S. Polo Open is held there every August.

The scoreboard at the Palm Beach
Polo and Country Club shows
the seven-minute clock and a close
game in the Cartier Open
tournament. The club, in
Wellington, Florida, has become a
center for the world's best high-
goal players, who compete from
December through April for high-
goal cups.

OPPOSITE: Peter Busch hits a
forehand drive at Palm Beach.

A groom braids tails at the pony lines in Eldorado, California.

LEFT: Players practice at the ground of the San Antonio Polo Club, in Retama, Texas. Founded in 1920, the club is one of the oldest in the U.S.

Héctor Barrantes (right) hooks sticks at Palm Beach. The head of Barrantes's stick has broken off during the stroke.

OPPOSITE: American teams attracted many international players such as Alfonso Pieres. Here playing for Peter Brant's team, White Birch Farm, at Palm Beach, Pieres leans out to strike the ball.

Peter Orthwein (right), playing for his team, Airstream, and Brad Scherer compete for the ball at Palm Beach.

RIGHT: Alan Connell and Steve Gose at the San Antonio Polo Club, Texas.

A groom leads four polo ponies off the ground at Broad Acres Polo Club, in Norman, Oklahoma.

LEFT: The handsome, well-appointed stables at the Wildwood Farms, in Memphis, Tennessee.

A holiday afternoon in the stands of Sotogrande, on the Costa del Sol, in southern Spain. The club holds tournaments on six grounds and has the largest concentration of polo players of any single club in Europe—eight high-goal teams, ten medium-goal teams, and six low-goal teams.

RIGHT: In May and June every year, the elegant polo club of Bagatelle, in the Bois de Boulogne, holds medium-goal tournaments that are also major events in the Paris social season.

At Pietermaritzburg, in the Republic of South Africa, polo teams compete in a haze of dust.

OPPOSITE: The umpire throws in the ball after a foul near the stands at the Santa Barbara Polo and Racquet Club, in California. Founded in 1911, the club is the third oldest in the U.S. and is a favorite of players for its pleasant climate and prestigious tournaments, the Pacific Coast Open and the America Cup.

Mickey Tarnopol, American patron and player for the Revlon team, after a strong forehand drive. Galloping up behind him is Federico Escobar, playing for White Birch Farm.

OPPOSITE: Memo Gracida and Héctor Galindo about to hook sticks in Palm Beach.

The Sultan of Pahang before a game.

OPPOSITE: The Sultan of Pahang's ponies in their pallets on deck, ready to be shipped to Brunei for a tournament.

The Sultan of Brunei with his brother Prince Mohammed.

RIGHT: An aerial photograph, taken in 1980, of the polo club and well-maintained grounds in Brunei also shows the rocky coastline of the island of Borneo, on the South China Sea. The sultan's keen interest in the game has developed Brunei into a leading international polo center.

A polo pony exercises with his trainer in the water at Kuala Lumpur, Malaysia. Carefully regulated swimming stimulates and heals strained muscles.

OPPOSITE: Polo ponies work out on the beach in Brunei. Salt water toughens up ponies' tendons.

Ponies are taken for daily swimming exercises in Santo Domingo, Dominican Republic.

OPPOSITE: Ponies enjoying the sea at Deauville.

A man on a ladder makes last-minute adjustments to the scoreboard at the start of a game in Nigeria.

OPPOSITE: A Nigerian groom in team colors, holding a pony with a matching braided mane, waits for a game to begin.

Ponies keep cool inside traditional adobe huts built as stables at the Kaduna Polo Club, in Nigeria.

OPPOSITE: Pony lines during a big tournament at the Kaduna Polo Club, in Nigeria.

A Sikh, in a dazzling yellow turban, prepares for a game in Delhi. Sikhs never wear helmets.

OPPOSITE: In the hills near Delhi, members of the Indian army's polo team train their ponies.

A wooden pony for practicing strokes stands in the courtyard of the palace, in Jaipur, India.

A player practices his swing on a wooden pony in Delhi.

OPPOSITE: An exotic form of polo can also be played from the back of an elephant. In Jaipur, elephants brilliantly decorated with powdered color carry a driver and a player.

Ponies amid cactus in Mexico
are rounded up at the *hacienda*
Rincón Gallardo, the country's
biggest pony-breeding center.

# Polo on the Estancia

A POLO PONY has to work at full tilt for seven and a half minutes and to stop dead whenever instructed. It has to turn sharply, gallop, ride off other ponies, cover distances again and again, all the while keeping its head. To perform consistently with different riders requires a well-trained animal. A true polo pony enjoys the game. I have seen many a pony watch a game attentively from the edge of the ground while waiting its turn to take part. I do not mean that ninety percent of polo depends on the pony, but I am tempted to say that this estimate is pretty close.

Thirty years ago polo ponies were small and were built close to the ground. Though larger ponies and even stallions have done well at the game, in my view, the smaller animal is more naturally agile. To be able to play flat out for a full chukker, a polo pony must be well proportioned and correct in its conformation. The most important aspect of a polo pony is its mouth. An animal with a good mouth enables a player to move around the ground with the confidence that he will be able to reach his shots, because he knows the pony is well schooled and well balanced. Another important feature is the animal's action. A low action is a relief to the player, for it guarantees that the

A groom rests with ponies in the shade of eucalyptus trees on an Argentine *estancia* in the summer.

pony will not make him strain at the crucial moment by an uneven gallop or prevent him from comfortably hitting the ball. A good pony pays attention when a player is making a stroke and allows him enough time.

The demands on the pony vary according to the player's position on the team. A number one is usually a fast, light player and requires a different kind of pony from a number four, who may be a player of heavier build, needing a more solid animal. A number two requires a strong, fast animal. The center, or pivot, of the team is number three, the most demanding position for both player and pony, because the fluctuations of the game require great adaptability. The number three pony sometimes gets a good gallop, but in most of the game it has to make short rushes with rapid changes of direction.

Breeding is partly an art form and partly a science. Through trial and error, the best breeders aim for—and sometimes reach—their ideal. Since the 1930s, Menditeguy, Alberdi, Dowling, Santamarina, Torres Zavaleta, Nelson, Harrington, and Barrantes have been justly famous names in this field. Along with many other breeders, these men have had an active influence on the improvement of the breed and in the success of the Argentine polo pony, which is recognized throughout the world.

In the past, because they could not continue to play while foaling, the reproductive period of polo-playing

At sunrise, Argentine polo ponies are driven from the fields to start their day of schooling and practice games.

mares was limited. They were not used for breeding until the age of twelve or fourteen, by which time it was hard to get them in foal. Today, as a result of embryo transfers, this has changed. The mare is artificially inseminated and, after seven days, the embryo is transferred to a receptor mare. Through this method a good mare can continue to play polo and, at the same time, be a mother to several foals. An Open champion polo pony can, therefore, produce many foals but will not be exhausted by long, eleven-month pregnancies. With this new method, there will be an increasing number of excellent quality polo ponies, and from now on the history of breeding polo ponies may well be divided into before and after the introduction of embryo transfers.

Every year, at the end of the Buenos Aires season, polo players go to the *estancias* for the summer to play the new ponies. Country polo is, I think, what makes Argentina so good at the sport and at riding. On long summer evenings, under a cloudless sky with a fresh breeze blowing across the plain, it is a pleasure to see a group of riders playing for fun, cantering about as they test their measure. The atmosphere is easygoing and friendly, and the nightly barbecues are unforgettable. Under the trees, firelight plays over the faces, while comments on the incidents of the day are exchanged.

El Pucará is an *estancia* in the southwest of the Province of Buenos Aires, about three hundred miles from

Every farm on the pampa raises beef cattle, and polo ponies can also be used to round them up and drive them into holding pens. It is excellent training for young animals.

the city of Buenos Aires. We bought our first acres there in 1974, and since then I have settled in Argentina and have developed an abiding love for the country. It was a great privilege to share that time with Héctor Barrantes, my late husband, an outstanding horseman, polo player, and great connoisseur of polo ponies. By his side, and in our daily life, I learned much about the breeding and schooling of ponies. For me, those years were an intensive course in the practical experience of ponies and have given me lasting memories. Because I am incurably left-handed I never played polo myself, but I rode all the new ponies to get them used to the game.

Héctor Barrantes loved to teach the young men who came to El Pucará. Every Saturday we would have a barbecue and discuss polo. "Before you hit the ball," he often repeated, "you must know where all the other seven players are. You have to use your back and shoulder to hit the ball. Remember that in a game you must always think one or two plays ahead and anticipate where the ball will go. Also, do not hit carelessly. The pony has to be in the air to hit under its neck. And when looking after ponies, remember that for them routine is essential." A most important duty for the boys who worked at El Pucará was to go out every morning with the groom and tame the foals. When a foal is five days old, it starts to wear a head collar, so that, as it is led around, it gradually becomes used to human handling. All the horse breakers who worked at El Pucará have told us that training our

Ponies are tied up at the *palenques*, or rails, waiting to be tacked up for a country polo game.

ponies was a pleasure, because half the work had already been done by the boys' careful handling.

Many young polo players did their early training at El Pucará. In all, there must have been some 250 boys who came to the farm to learn the routine and the secrets of the game. Charles Beresford was one of the people who helped us in the early days, when El Pucará was being built. He is still a great friend, and his help at that time, when we had neither light nor running water, was invaluable. Today he continues his brilliant career in Chile. Andrew MacDonald, of Australia, came to work for us for six months and stayed for three years. Anthony Fanshawe and Nicholas Manifold first started playing polo at El Pucará, and today both play off a five-goal handicap. Nicholas plays in the United States with Peter Brant and manages White Birch Farm; Anthony plays in England and Argentina. There was also Tod Offen, a Canadian, who is now a seven-goaler. Other Argentine friends of many years, who came to the farm as young players and are memorable not only as players but as people who understand everything about ponies, include Gonzalo Pieres, Martín Zubía, and Mariano Aguerre.

Juan José Boote deserves special mention as a rider, as one of the best trainers in Argentina, and as one of the very few people who know how to train a top-class pony to perfection. He has an inborn talent and can bring out an animal's best features. Héctor's pony Luna owes much of her world success to the love and care that Boote

Ponies are returned to the fields at the end of each day.

continued to give her from her first days of polo right through her career until she stopped playing in 1995. Along with Claudio Pérez, Boote made more ponies of high quality with and for Héctor than anyone else at El Pucará. Claudio Pérez, now a three-goaler, made Héctor's winning pony Pelusita.

It is an unbelievably rewarding feeling to see your breed performing at Palermo. Héctor won many important prizes with his ponies. In 1986, his pony Cachamai won the Susan Townley Cup, at Palermo, a prize for the best-playing pony in the Argentine Open, and Luna repeated the feat the following year. In 1990, three of Héctor's ponies won top prizes throughout the world. Pelusita won the best-playing pony in England at Smith's Lawn, Windsor; Levicú won the best-playing pony in the United States, at Palm Beach; and Luna won the best-playing pony in Argentina, at Palermo. Héctor died that year, in August, and these ponies were his last great joys.

Héctor and Susan Barrantes in the fields at El Pucará.

A traditional method of training in Argentina uses a *madrina*, or godmother horse, with a bell around her neck, to help break the two-year-old *potros*, or colts. Here the *domador*, or breaker, leads the bell mare in from the fields along with the colts, who have learned to follow her.

Juan Carlos Pérez, age three, Claudio Pérez's son, starts his polo career early.

Young players and ponies ride to the ground to play the first chukkers of a country game.

OPPOSITE: Saddles and blankets are draped over the rails of a *palenque* in the shade on a hot summer's day.

Grooms relax under the trees before a game.

OPPOSITE: Claudio Pérez schools a new pony. After being broken, four-year old ponies are trained to get used to the swinging of mallets, to stop short in the middle of a fast run, and to enjoy playing the game up close with other ponies.

An *Asado*, the traditional Argentine barbecue, is the favorite open-air meal in the summer. Grass-fed cattle produce a full-flavored beef, which is a staple part of the national diet. A barbecue typically includes sausages and many different parts of the animal, including ribs, steaks, and sweetbreads. Here groom Osvaldo Pineda enjoys his barbecue at knife point.

RIGHT: Héctor Barrantes's best stallion, Sequito.

A groom braids a pony's tail before a game.

RIGHT: A young foal gradually gets used to being handled and is easier to break when it has had plenty of human contact.

*Acknowledgments*

I should like to express my thanks to H.R.H. The Prince of Wales for his foreword to this book and to Juan Carlos Harriot for the introduction.

I am additionally grateful to the friends and associates who encouraged me to compile the book and assisted in its production, in particular the staffs of the Argentine Polo Association and of SB Producciones S.A.

Thanks are also due to the photographers Yann Arthus-Bertrand, Jonathan Becker, and Reto Guntli for their generous contributions as well as to all the other photographers and friends who went to great lengths to provide me with useful material. And, finally, a special thought to Mari.

S.B.

# Index of Names

*Photographs are indicated by bold-face page numbers.*

# POLO

by Susan Barrantes
with the collaboration of Jorge Torres Zavaleta

Published by Ediciones Larivière S. A.,
Talcahuano 768, (1013) Buenos Aires, Argentina
Project coordination: Baroness Francesca von Thielmann

First edition
Printed by Arnoldo Mondadori in Italy
Color separations: Quadrilaser

Design: Marcus Ratliff
Editing: Jenifer Ratliff
Composition: Amy Pyle
Text consultants: Susan Ashe and
Norman Thomas di Giovanni